GOLF MADE EASY

GOLF
MADE EASY

JOHNNY M. ANDERSON

A & C Black • London

First published in 1992 by
A & C Black (Publishers) Limited
35 Bedford Row, London WC1R 4JH

World copyright © 1992 Streiffert & Co
Box 5334, S-102 46 Stockholm, Sweden.

ISBN 0 7136 3407 3

Idea, editorial and production: Johnston Editions,
Gothenburg, Sweden

Photography: David Jeffery

Design and page make-up: Streiffert & Co

A CIP catalogue record for this book is available from the British
Library

Colour reproduction: Repro-Man, Gothenburg, Sweden
Printed in Italy by arrangement with Graphicom S.r.l., Vicenza

CONTENTS

INTRODUCTION 6

Chapter 1: EQUIPMENT AND GEOMETRY FOR THE GOLFER 9

Chapter 2: PUTTING 19

Chapter 3: GOLFING BASICS 41

Chapter 4: CHIPPING 59

Chapter 5: PITCHING 73

Chapter 6: THE PARTIAL SWING 85

Chapter 7: THE FULL SWING 93

Chapter 8: THE SAND GAME 113

Chapter 9: RECOVERY SHOTS FROM THE ROUGH 131

AFTERWORD 140

INDEX 144

INTRODUCTION

No matter what anybody else says to you, you play golf to enjoy yourself and have fun out there on the course. No more, no less. The more you improve, the more you will enjoy yourself. And remember, it is against the course and your own handicap that you play, not against your golf partners.

The object of the game of golf is to play the course on any given day under the prevailing circumstances in the lowest possible number of shots, while you are really enjoying yourself.

You can improve your game!
Everybody can improve their game. Thirty-five years spent teaching golf to beginners, high- and low-handicap golfers, international players, and professionals, have taught me that. Another thing those years have taught me is that practice does not make perfect, but that only *intelligent* practice will improve your game and your

enjoyment of it. Furthermore, my experience is that there is no substitute for good tuition, so this book is intended to be a complement to the lessons you get from your pro. It can be used also at any time to refresh your memory and to help you improve your scoring.

The more you learn about golf, the greater your understanding of the game; the more you understand, the greater your golfing confidence; and the more confident you are about your golf, the greater are your chances of success. This book is a step-by-step approach to building up a solid golf game and will help you to improve by taking one step at a time, never moving forwards until the previous step has been understood, practised and mastered.

Step by step

This book is designed to help all those golf players who are not satisfied with the way their game is developing. Beginners will find that the easy-to-follow photographs and instructions will be an excellent aid when they are going through the basics or want to refresh their minds on lessons they have received from their golf instructor. More experienced players will be able to refer to the relevant section when they find that a particular part of their game seems to have deteriorated.

The aim is to help you to build up and improve your game step by step, starting with putting and then going through chipping, pitching, the half swing, the three-quarter swing, and finally the full swing. Do not go on to a new section before you are sure that the previous one has been understood and practised success-fully, thus giving you the confidence to break new ground.

Don't make it so difficult!

Golf must be the most frustrating and difficult ball game devised, so you should always try to keep it as simple as possible. All beginners and even those who have played for a considerable time have a tendency to make it more difficult than it really is. The reasons for this follow.

1 Lack of understanding: you don't quite know what you are trying to do with your golf swing. The object of the golf swing is to strike the ball with the club face and swing path pointing at the target at the moment of impact. No more, no less.

2 Bad memory or loss of emotional control: you forget your all-important pre-swing routine or you get angry at or frightened by a particular situation.

3 You try too hard: inexperienced weekend players try to imitate the speed, agility and strength of the tournament players who practise and play every day.

4 Not enough intelligent practice: after a golf lesson from your pro, you prefer to get out on the course and play badly than to stay in the practice area and improve your game by intelligent practice.

Practice

Playing high- or middle-handicap golf has as little to do with professional tournament golf as driving a family car in town has to do with Formula 1 racing. Professional tournament golfers are top athletes and are not easily copied. They practise and play regularly. When they practise, they work at one particular aspect of their game, concentrating on one type of shot only, taking their time at it, and noting the results.

High-handicap players usually practise with the wooden clubs, and to the bystander they sometimes look like windmills trying to hit as many balls as possible into the air at the same time. When you practise, start with your shorter shots and take your time. Consider each shot you take and try to work out why it went the way it did. Write it down in a notebook that you should always have with you. Then at the end of the session, summarise the results of your practice shots, so that you can refer to them at the start of your next practice session.

CHAPTER ONE
EQUIPMENT AND GEOMETRY FOR THE GOLFER

As we are all built differently, golf clubs are particularly individual and should be chosen with care. A club that does not suit your style of play or your physical ability will make it very difficult for you to improve at the game. There are many different shaft flexes and club-head weights to choose from; if you are a normal weekend golfer or middle-handicapper, you are simply not knowledgeable enough to choose for yourself. Instead, turn to the golf pro who has had the privilege of teaching you – there is no better person to help you choose clubs that are right for you, your physique, your style of playing, and the degree of improvement that he or she expects you to attain.

THE CLUBS

As a rule, stiff-shafted and heavy-headed clubs are best left to the strong and experienced playing professionals. You, as a high- or medium-handicapper, need clubs that will give you a better chance of making a high percentage of good golf shots, while giving you the best possible results from your bad shots.

According to the rules of golf, you may not play with more than fourteen clubs in your bag, and professionals always choose their fourteen to suit the prevailing weather conditions and the particular course to be played.

The beginner will probably improve faster if he or she uses only the Nos 3, 5 and 7 woods and the Nos 5, 7 and 9 irons, the pitching wedge, the sand iron and the putter. Using the full set before you are experienced enough will only be confusing and will lead to uncertainty and lack of confidence.

Which club to use?

The use of the clubs is fairly obvious. The longer-shafted clubs send the ball further. The woods are for shots from the tee or for the 'transport' shots that should leave you with a simple shot on to the green, close to the flag. The No. 3 wood is used from the tee, while the Nos 5 and 7 woods are for play on the fairway or for par 3 tee shots. Shots hit with these clubs allow you a greater margin of error – for instance, ball side-spin will be less than with the driver, so there will be a minimum loss of line (direction) and length.

The middle irons are for playing the ball on to the green with a reasonable amount of accuracy. The No. 5 iron is the longest iron the high-handicapper can use with any accuracy, so leave the longer irons until you can handle them properly.

Use the shorter clubs when accuracy is at a premium; in other words, when you want to send the ball higher and shorter to land on the green. The pitching wedge (or 'wedge', as it is also known) is for play near

the green, while the sand iron is, as the name indicates, for playing from sand, but it is also a useful weapon when you need to get out of troublesome rough or when you need extra height to your shot. Finally, the putter is for playing the ball in the vicinity of the flag.

Here I have placed the clubs correctly in their bag, which is big enough to hold extra clothing and other necessities. I always keep the woods protected with head covers.

Opposite is my present set of clubs:
three woods (Nos 1, 3 and 5), nine irons (Nos 3 – 9, a pitching wedge and a sand iron), and one putter. You will notice that the more lofted the club, the shorter the shaft.

Accessories

A bag with plenty of space for extra clothing, a water bottle, and perhaps a refreshing snack (a sandwich and some fruit) is a sound investment. A smaller bag, for carrying a reduced number of clubs, is also a good buy. The big bag can be used when you play a full round with a complete set of clubs. It is then a good idea to have a trolley for your bag, since walking 4–5 miles (6–8 km) and playing golf is tiring enough without having to carry a heavy bag. The small bag will serve for playing just a few holes in the evening or when you go to the practice area.

Whether you use a golf glove is a matter of personal preference. The majority of professionals wear golf gloves except when putting. Many players find that it gives them a better grip and, therefore, increased confidence during the swing.

The type of golf shoes you choose will depend on what type of course you play most frequently, but whatever kind of shoes you have, keep them in good condition. Replace worn spikes and fit shoe trees when you are not using your shoes. If you play a good deal of golf, it is wise to have two pairs of shoes in order to allow one pair to 'rest up' while you are using the other. If you play in a rainy climate, a pair of rubber golf boots is a boon, keeping your feet and legs dry, especially if you spend plenty of time in the rough.

Buy twenty or thirty practice balls of good quality for practising your chipping and putting, because driving-range balls do not generate the correct sensation felt when playing good shots around and on the green.

The best teacher

Let me now introduce you to the finest and most honest golf teacher in the world. It is *always* with you when you are playing, it cannot lie, and it does only what you tell it to, without asking questions. This trustworthy teacher is none other than your golf ball. It can do only what is achieved with your influence. If you strike it cleanly using a full swing, it will do one of nine things in relation to the target line, and it will never do anything else. The target line is the imaginary line that runs back from the target through the ball; we will refer to the target line frequently throughout this book, so if this basic definition is not already firmly imprinted on your mind, make a point of imprinting it now. The nine ball-flight alternatives are the following.

1 The ball will fly in a straight line towards the target.

2 It will fly in a straight line to the left of the target. This is known as a **pull**.

3 It will fly in a straight line to the right of the target. This is a **push**.

4 It will start off straight and then curve slightly to the left. A **draw**.

5 It will start off straight and then curve slightly to the right. A **fade**.

6 It will start off to the left of the target line and then curve to the right. A **pull-slice**.

7 It will start off to the left of the target line and then curve even more to the left. A **pull-hook**.

8 It will start off to the right of the target line and then curve to the left. A **push-hook**.

9 It will start off to the right of the target line and then curve even more to the right. A **push-slice**.

Swing path at impact

According to the coaching books, points 1 to 3 above indicate the effect of the club head's swing path at impact. The swing path is the line followed by the club head during the swing and it is always referred to in relation to the target line. The correct swing path is in-to-along-to-in, that is from the inside (your side) of the target line on the downswing, along the target line just before and after impact, and then back inside the target line on the upswing/follow through. Any other swing path will not start the ball off on a straight line towards the target.

The alignment of the club face at impact

The coaching books also tell you that a ball that curves after starting off straight indicates that the swing path was correct. However, the club face at impact was not square to the target line, but either open or closed to varying degrees (points 4 and 5). Points 6 to 9 are all caused by club faces that were not square to the swing path at impact. The fact that the ball did not start straight at the target tells you that the swing path was incorrect.

The angle of approach of the club head to the ball

Furthermore, the coaching books will tell you, the steepness of the downswing (the angle at which the club face approaches the ball) will affect the length and height of the ball's flight. A ball struck by a club head that is approaching too steeply will lose some length and gain more height than if it was hit by a club head swinging down at the normal angle of approach. If we add to this a club face that is open, the ball will fly even higher.

Cause and effect

So, how does the ordinary golfer learn the ins and outs of ball-flight laws without taking out a degree in Golf Engineering? Don't be put off by the technicalities; it is basically quite straightforward. The important thing is to think of the golf swing as a simple cause-and-effect phenomenon (your swing will cause an effect on the ball, i.e. it will make it do one of the nine things listed above). The table at the bottom of the page will show you this cause-and-effect approach more simply.

Whenever your shot does not succeed in making the ball finish up where you wanted it to go, you know that you have done something wrong. The flight of the ball shows you what it was that you did, so you can then concentrate on correcting the error (or errors). How to do this is described on p. 141.

EFFECT	CAUSE
1 The ball flies in a straight line towards the target.	You have done everything right unless you didn't want to hit that ball straight towards the target! In other words, the swing path was from the inside of the target line to along it at impact and then back inside, with the club face square at impact.
2 It flies in a straight line to the left of the target.	You have done everything right except that the club face travelled from outside the target line on the downswing to inside the target line on the follow through (known as out-to-in).
3 It flies in a straight line to the right of the target.	You have done everything right except that the club face travelled on a path that went from inside the target line on the downswing to outside the target line on the follow through (known as an in-to-out swing path).
4 It starts off straight to the target and then curves to the left.	You have swung the club to the target but the club face was closed at impact.
5 It starts off straight to the target and then curves to the right.	You have swung the club to the target but the club face was open at impact.
6 It starts off to the left of the target line and then curves back to the right.	This time, your swing path was out-to-in and the club face was open to the swing path at impact. Two things to correct!
7 It starts off to the left of the target line and then curves more to the left.	Your swing path was out-to-in and the club face was closed to the swing path at impact. Again, two things to correct.
8 It starts off to the right of the target line and then curves back to the left.	Your swing path was in-to-out and the club face was closed to the swing path at impact. Two things to correct.
9 It starts off to the right of the target line and then curves to the right.	Your swing path was in-to-out and the club face was open to the swing path at impact. Two things to correct.

2. Even the grip is different. Its shape is different and the part on which you place your thumbs is flattened and thickened towards the top, enabling you to hold the club in a manner designed to increase precision. Also, the material of the grip is different – it gives a softer 'feel'.

3. If you place the head of the putter flat on the ground beside that of any other club, you will see that the putter head is much nearer your feet and the shaft more upright, enabling you to stand closer to the ball.

4. How to find the sweet spot. Hold the shaft near the head and tap it with a tee, starting at the toe and working your way towards the heel. When the club head no longer twists but swings back and forwards, you have found the sweet spot.

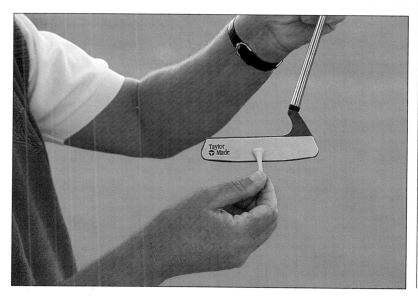

THE PUTTING GRIP

There are several ways of holding a putter and most golf players have, at some time in their golfing lives, tried some of them in an attempt to improve their putting. We show three of the most usual grips here. Each golfer should pick the grip that feels most comfortable and gives the best results.

The reverse overlap grip
This is the most usual grip. Hold the putter mainly with the last three fingers of each hand, with the left hand nearer the top of the shaft. The forefinger of the left hand is placed outside the last three fingers of the right hand. Three things should then point straight at the target: the back of the left hand, the face of the club head, and the palm of the right hand. This position helps to reduce wrist movement while allowing the arms to control the amount and direction of the movement. If your putting is causing you problems, it may be because your wrists are still hingeing; counteract this by turning the hands away from one another a little.

The standard grip, used by most players, is known as the reverse overlap grip.

The reverse overlap grip

1. Hold the very top of the putter in your right hand with the full area of its sole in contact with the ground and the shaft upright or even forward.

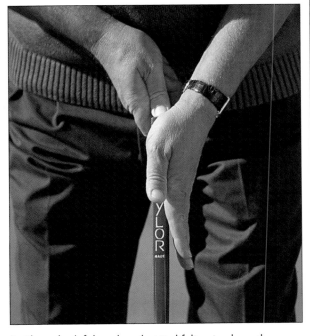

2. Place the left hand so that its lifeline is along the leading edge of the shaft. The back of the left hand should then point in the same direction as the club face.

Putting from off the green

1. The ball is on the foregreen, about 3 ft (1m) from the edge of the green, with a further 25 ft (8m) to the hole, which lies slightly downhill: a typical situation in which you should choose the putter, because with a lofted club you risk sending the ball too far.

2. Follow your usual putting routine, with those all-important practice swings to give you the right feeling for the swing required.

3. When addressing the ball, lean to the left, with the weight on your left foot and the hands well in front of the ball. Play the shot normally.

4. A satisfactory result: the ball finishes just past the hole, leaving an easy uphill putt. A shot has been saved, using common sense, imagination and your putter.

THE COMPLETE PUTTING GAME

Putting is that part of the game that is most variable. Sometimes, putts are missed for no apparent reason, causing loss of confidence and soaring scores. Do not allow this kind of situation to continue – something must be done.

Start by improving your reading of the green. For instance, it is worth noting that greens tend to lean away from high ground and towards the sea (if playing on a seaside course). Allow for slightly more slope than you think there actually is. The shorter the grass is cut, the longer the ball will roll and the more it will be affected by the slope; you must take this into account.

The nap of the green (the direction in

direction, it will be dull and dark (often called 'red') and the ball will stop much quicker. Therefore, you need a longer backswing to achieve the same distance.

Then create a putting routine that will be a constant factor in your putting game. As mentioned previously, routine will help you to concentrate, thus preventing your thoughts from leaving the job at hand and wandering – for instance, starting to worry about missing. Your routine will also create confidence, based on the feeling that you have made the right decision about line and the length of backswing. You must believe that what you are about to do will be successful.

Occasionally, it is impossible to find a suitable intermediate target, or you may even find one and lose it when standing to the ball. You must then use your imagination to help you stick to the decision that you have already made.

Strike the ball with the sweet spot, using the arms to create a smooth flowing movement, allowing the putter to move freely. Do not be over-mechanical or try to over-control the movement while making the stroke.

Make a habit of practising your putting routine: first, inspecting the pace and slope of the green before deciding on line and length, seeing always a successful result before taking up your stance. Then strike the ball immediately and with authority. Don't change your mind, and above all, stand still. Practise with a friend, competing with each other to create the atmosphere you will meet out on the course.

At some stage, if you have taken too many shots to reach the green, you may lose interest in finishing well, thus increasing your score even more. Remember that every shot has the same value. A good putt will put you in a more confident mood for the next hole.

Good putting seems to do something no other shot can do – it not only helps to keep your scores low, but it also makes the rest of the game a little easier and considerably more enjoyable.

You can't sink them all!

which the grass is cut and growing) will affect the speed of the ball. If the grass along which your ball will roll is cut away from you, it will be bright and shiny (green). The ball will roll faster and take longer to stop. Therefore, this putt needs less backswing.

If the grass has been cut in the other

CHAPTER THREE
GOLFING BASICS

The way you hold the club determines the position of the club head at impact, which in turn decides the direction, height and length of the shot. So don't regard your grip as simply a contact between you and the shaft of the club, because it is of primary importance to the result of the swing. How you hold the club is quite personal, due to the shape and size of your hands, so every golfer's swing is unique, despite the fact that all golf swings must attempt to do the same thing!

HOW TO HOLD THE CLUB

There are several different ways of holding the club, the most normal being the Vardon grip, also known as the overlapping grip, in which the little finger of the right hand overlaps the forefinger of the left. We illustrate three types of grip here.

Whatever grip you choose to use, remember that it should be firm and light, with most of the pressure coming from the last three fingers of the left hand and the middle two of the right.

With the hands in this position, they form a unit in which they work together. Should the V-shape between the respective forefingers and thumbs not be parallel, the hands will work independently, so the club face will be incorrect at impact. Remember:

* V-shapes parallel
* hands together
* firm but light and constant pressure from the last three fingers of the left and the two middle fingers of the right hand.

Holding the club too tightly will cause tension and greatly reduce the free flowing movement of the swing, causing crooked shots and lack of distance.

As your game improves and your swing grows stronger, you may need to change the position of your hands. However, as a beginner or high-handicapper, you should use the above hand positions. Adjustments may be necessary from time to time during your golfing career, either to re-discover that straight ball flight or to learn how to curve the ball in the air. If the hands are moved left on the shaft, the ball will tend to curve to the right, and vice versa. But all such changes to your grip should be discussed with your golf professional before you start to attempt them seriously.

The Harry Vardon grip

1. *The left hand first.* Be sure that the club head is placed correctly on the ground, with the club face square, pointing directly forwards. It should not be open (to the right) or closed (to the left). With your right hand at the top of the grip, hold the club steady so that the club face doesn't move off the target line. Now place the left hand so that it lies diagonally on the shaft from where the forefinger joins the palm to the underside of the pad at the base of your hand. Your left arm should be fairly straight.

leading edge at right angles to a line running from the ball to the intermediate target. The two vertical lines of the face of the iron clubs will help you do this. Only then do you take your stance, first putting your right foot in position and then the left. Take care not to bring the club head out of alignment with the intermediate target. In other words, position the club first and then position yourself with reference to the club. Check that the club head is aligned with the intermediate target before looking towards the actual target.

Align your club head to the intermediate target every time you prepare to take a shot, so that it becomes an automatic part of your routine. This not only helps shot making but also makes it much easier to align feet and body.

The vast majority of golfers tend to aim first with the feet and then with the club face. This always results in the aim being far to the right of the target. The natural reaction to this is to try to change the swing path and the position of the club face in order to correct a faulty aim, thus complicating matters even further. Therefore, you must be sure that the club face is positioned correctly *before* you take your stance.

Target line

Picking the intermediate target, as just shown, is extremely important. However, it is also vital that you are aware of the target line, which runs in a straight line through the ball and the intermediate target.

1. Part of the target line is marked out here by a strip of white tape. It helps you to adopt the correct posture and stance. Eyeline, shoulders, knees and feet must be parallel to the target line.

2. The ball is struck first and then the tape and ground, taking a little divot. The club head then moves back inside the target line and up to the finish position. Being aware of the target line will also assist you to keep the club head on the proper swing path (*see* pp. 54 – 5).

When practising your aim, lay down a club 3 in (75 mm) outside the ball and pointing at the target. The two occasions when your club head is nearest to the shaft of the club on the ground should be at address and at impact. Another club can be laid in line with your toes, to ensure that you are standing parallel when playing the complete swing movement. Good aiming will assist you to swing the club towards the target and not only at the ball.

THE POSITION OF THE BALL

The position of the ball in the stance varies from individual to individual. Top professionals with magnificent hand and leg action favour a constant ball position, well forward in the stance (nearer the left foot). We mortals, however, need to vary the position of the ball to suit our level of prowess. On the opposite page, we give some guidelines.

STANCE

Adopting the correct stance is easier if you have aimed the club head correctly, using the intermediate target as a guide. When the club is properly aimed, the club face is pointing along the target line at the intermediate target. Then place your feet, first the right and then the left, so that they are at right angles to the target line. In other words, a line drawn from your left toe to your right toe would be parallel with the target line.

Because your swing should be shorter the nearer you are to the green, withdraw your left foot from the line to prevent slackness creeping into the swing movement and to allow each part of your body to move in the correct sequence during the swing.

Normally, the longer the swing you intend to take, the wider the distance between your feet and the more weight

Aim

No matter how well you swing your club, you won't achieve the desired result if you have not aimed properly. Correct aiming is a matter of high priority, and to achieve this you must use an intermediate target (*see* p. 46).

1. Place the club head behind the ball, so that the club face is pointing directly at the intermediate target.

2. Take your stance, making sure not to move the club head in relation to the intermediate target while you are arranging the position of your feet and body.

Practising the aim and stance
Place one club on the ground just on the far side of the ball, and another just in front of your feet. Both clubs should be parallel with the target line and when you stand to the ball, your eyes, shoulders, hips and feet should also be parallel to those clubs.

you have on your right foot when you address the ball.

Always follow the same routine: club head behind the ball and aimed correctly at the intermediate target; then the right foot in position, followed by the left.

For the complete swing movement, with the ball suitably placed, you will find that by 'softening' (holding it less tensely) and bending your right elbow, your right shoulder will be lower than your left. This will bring your head and upper body in the correct position behind the ball. Be sure, however, that your body alignment is still correct. Everything – that is feet, knees, hips, shoulders and (equally important) eyeline – should be parallel to the target line. You may turn your head slightly to the right, giving the impression you are looking at the back of the ball with your left eye, but the eyeline must not deviate from the parallel.

Stance

Experiment with various ball positions to establish the correct ones for your personal swing. A good rule of thumb is that when the club head is correctly placed and pointing at the intermediate target, the shaft should be pointing directly at your left groin.

So, place your club head behind the ball, aimed at the intermediate target, then position your feet, and finally check that the rest of your body is aligned properly.

For short irons – a centred ball.
Place your feet so that the ball is centred between them. This gives the club head a steeper approach to the ball on the downswing and helps to give the shot height and back-spin. (*Right*)

For the medium/long irons – forward in the stance.
Place your feet so that the ball is more forward in the stance (closer to your left foot). This gives the club head a more shallow approach to the ball, making the ball fly further.

For the woods from the tee – inside the left heel.
Place your feet so that the ball is just inside the left heel. This causes you to strike the ball on the upswing, after the swing has reached the lowest point of its arc, producing a shot that starts on a low trajectory and results in maximum length.

The different ball positions can be seen easily here. The shorter irons require the ball to be nearer the feet and centred or slightly to the right of centre. As the shaft increases in length, the ball should be increasingly nearer the left foot. As the ball is already in position, you must position your body to the ball, not vice versa!

PRE-SHOT ROUTINE

We have already described pre-shot routine in the previous chapter, in which the art of putting was discussed. Pre-shot routine for all the other shots is basically the same – the most important aspect of your routine is that it is always the same! The key is that you are reminding yourself about all the vital elements of your golf shot: examining the lie of the ball, choosing the club, picking out the intermediate target, and playing your practice swings while seeing in your mind's eye a successful result of those practice swings. You are encouraging your mind to conjure up the feeling of coming to terms with the shot you are about to play – you have played this kind of shot well before and by going through the same pre-shot routine you are encouraging a repeat of that successful shot.

Follow your routine!
So, what you do prior to making your stroke and the order in which you do it is an essential part of your golf swing. All good players have a pattern or routine that they always follow.

First they look at the lie of the ball and then the target area, before they choose the club. Then they hold the club in the correct grip and pick out the intermediate target.

If the swing is a partial movement, they take a couple of practice swings, aiming at the target and imagining a successful flight and roll of the ball. Should it be a full swing movement, they take a 'mini-swing' to establish swing rhythm and get rid of unwanted tension in the arms. Only then is the club head placed behind the ball, with the club face pointing at the intermediate target.

The stance is taken, the right foot being positioned before the left. Then the feet are finally adjusted as the player checks his posture and alignment. The head swivels towards the target, imagining all the while the flight, bounce and roll of the ball,

terminating in a successful result. The head is not *turned* towards the target, as this could cause a change of shoulder position. Instead, it is *swivelled*, the right eye being lower than the left when looking along the target line.

The position of the club face is again checked, before the eyes are focussed on the back of the ball, but with the target still firmly in the mind's eye. The player then takes a constant number of waggles, and continues into the forward press which starts the backswing.

Some professionals even place the club behind the ball before taking their grip, but whatever you do be sure that your routine is always the same and should you be disturbed and lose your concentration, stop, and start again.

Important!
Although you are looking at the back of the ball, you should be seeing the ball flight in your mind's eye. This will encourage you to swing the club to the target and not only to the ball. Furthermore, your practice swings are a preparation for the swing to come and should be done at a similar speed as the actual swing. Purposeful, yes, but still leisurely. While your mind is thus engaged and relaxed by your usual routine, your concentration is sharp and remains on the job at hand, with no increase in your level of tension.

The pre-shot routine should move you smoothly into the start of the backswing with constant motion. Standing still over the ball will only cause increased tension.

Pre-shot routine

Your pre-shot routine has two goals: to put you in a confident frame of mind and to put your body in the correct stance, with good alignment every time. The series of photos shows practising from the fairway with the No. 9 iron and using a ball as the intermediate target.

1. First of all, one or two half swings to get the feeling of the club head 'freewheeling' through the hitting area. Always make the same number of practice swings.

2. The club head is placed behind the ball, aligned at the intermediate target.

3. The stance is then taken. Check the alignment of the club head to the intermediate target (has it changed since the previous step, when you aligned it?) and that the upper body is parallel to the target line.

POSTURE

Posture is the positioning of the body during the golf swing and is an element that the weekend golfer often neglects, to the detriment of his or her golf swing. In all good swings, the golfer leans forwards from the waist, with the shoulders relaxed and the arms hanging freely. This helps produce a free and unrestricted movement that makes for greater club-head speed and well struck shots of appreciable length. Any body tension during address is immediately reflected in loss of rhythm, which affects the strike and the length of the shot. Keep your back fairly straight and, with the longer clubs, the lower spine should be almost parallel to the line formed between the heels and the back of the knees. Good posture allows for a freer, more complete movement and reduces tension.

Because the right elbow is slightly bent and the right hand is below the left on the shaft, lower the right shoulder, otherwise the upper body would point far too much to the left, restricting your backswing.

For the longer shots the weight is predominantly on the balls of the feet and the greater the distance required, the more your weight should favour the right foot.

Flex the knees to assist good balance and weight transference, which will occur naturally during the swing if your set-up and alignment are correct. The right knee is inclined to the left in order to prevent the upper body from swaying. This puts weight on the inside of the right foot, enabling you to turn around the right hip.

The head and upper body are significantly behind the ball; they are increasingly further behind the longer the club you use.

Posture

The tee-shot posture is shown here. Note how the arms are hanging freely from the shoulders, with the hands inside the eyeline, and the body bent forwards from the waist.

The knees are slightly flexed and everything is parallel to the target line: feet, knees, hips, shoulders and – very important – the eyeline.

Note also how the right shoulder is lower than the left, and how the right elbow is bent and nearer the body than the left.

It is from this position that the backswing should move quite naturally into the correct path and plane.

FORWARD PRESS

Smoothness of swing movement is a prerequisite if you want to improve your golf – and who doesn't? – and nowhere is it more necessary and difficult than at the start of the backswing. If you start the backswing from a completely stationary hand position, there is a great danger of jerking the club head back from the ball, resulting in bad timing and often a radical change of the position of the club face at impact. The forward press will help you initiate the backswing smoothly on all your golf shots, including putting. When putting or playing short shots from around the green, the forward press is made by inclining the shaft forwards towards the target very slightly, a movement carried out only by the forearms immediately prior to starting the backswing.

With the longer shots, also move your right knee inwards towards the left, enabling the club to 'rebound' smoothly into the backswing.

N.B. When making the forward press, take care to do it gently so as not to touch the ball.

The forward press

The forward press leads to the start of the backswing and ensures that you don't jerk the club head away from the ball, but rather move it smoothly back.

The forward movement of the club rebounds softly into the backswing, so as to start the swing with a fluid motion.

1. The normal address position, with the hands over the ball and the shaft of the club pointing at the left groin.

2. The hands press forwards slightly until they are just in front of the ball, and the right knee moves forwards before rebounding smoothly into the backswing.

SWING PATH

A correct aim, stance, posture and mental picture of the desired flight will certainly encourage the correct swing path. The arms are swung back away from the ball and as the shoulders are pulled round by the arms, the club moves slightly to the inside and then up. So, the backswing line is *back-in-up*. On the way down, the arms are swung down with the club head approaching the ball from the inside of the target line, before swinging along the line at impact. (Not in-to-out and not out-to-in, but *down to the inside* and *along the target*

Swing path

I illustrate the path followed by the club head with the help of a thick length of black rubber that I have been using successfully for years.

The fact that one always stands to the side of the ball means that the club head can only be swung directly at the target for a very short part of the swing path. The club head moves not only back and up and down and forwards, but it also moves around the body, as illustrated.

1. The club head moves straight back from the ball and has already started to move inside.

2. It continues to move more to the inside at the same time as it begins to move up...

3. ...to a position in which the club shaft is parallel to the target line.

4. Then back down, somewhat more on the inside (compare this with photo 2).

CHAPTER FOUR
CHIPPING

In the chip-and-run shot the ball spends the minimum amount of time in the air and the maximum amount of time on the ground. The shot is used to play a ball from the foregreen or the fairway on to the green and close to the hole. The shot to play and the club to choose are dictated by the lie of the ball and the fact that the intervening ground is unsuitable for the use of the putter.

The chip-and-run shot with the right club will get the ball into the air at the correct height, fly it over the foregreen, land it gently on the front edge of the green, and roll it to the flag. The stance and posture will help to create a descending blow, causing the ball to roll up the club face and producing the required height without the use of the hands or wrists.

THE SHORT CHIP-AND-RUN SHOT

The short chip-and-run shot is, like the putting stroke, a one-lever movement. If played correctly, it gives great accuracy.

The two-lever movement (arms and wrists) is used when greater height and length are required. This movement is described later in this chapter, where we cover the long chip-and-run.

The choice of club
The club you need to make this shot can vary from a No. 4 iron to a sand iron. The correct choice will depend on the following factors.

1 *The lie of the ball.* Is it a good lie (sitting neatly on top of the grass), is it lying on hard, bare ground, or is it nestling in the grass of the semi-rough?

2 *The distance to the edge of the green.* Always allow for a safety margin, so that a shot struck with less than 100% will still carry the intervening ground and land on the putting surface.

3 *The distance from the landing point to the flag, and the condition and slope of the green.* The example opposite will make it easier to understand. The ball is about 3 ft (1 m) from the edge of the green, which slopes away from you and is medium-paced. The flag is 33 ft (10 m) from the edge. The ball is lying well, but there is some longer grass between it and the green, preventing you from using the safest club, the putter.

You want the ball to clear the uncut grass on a low trajectory to land about 6 ft (2 m) into the green. In other words, it must fly 9 ft (3 m) before bouncing a couple of times and rolling the remaining 27 ft (8 m) to the flag. As the flag is down the slope, you should try to get the ball to stop slightly past the hole, as an uphill putt is easier.

You know from previous experience that a No. 7 or 8 iron should do the job, *if* you use a movement similar to that for the long putt.

As far as the movement is concerned, the normal chip-and-run shot reminds us of the putting stroke, the only difference being that the ball leaves the ground because the irons are built differently than the putter. On the club face there are a number of grooves, two vertical and eight to ten horizontal. The vertical grooves help you to aim the club, while the horizontal ones create back-spin and control.

The angle of the iron club's shaft to its head is flatter, so you must stand a little further away from the ball than you would if you were using the putter. For shots of this type, hold the club further down the shaft with your normal grip (for instance, the Vardon grip), because the grip on the iron club is round, not flattened like the putter.

The No. 7 iron has approximately a 35° loft, so to strike the ball correctly hit it at its base and just before the club head has reached its lowest point (just before making contact with the grass). The same amount of movement with a No. 4 iron would send the ball on a lower trajectory and roll it past the flag; with a No. 9 iron or a wedge, the ball would have increased height but would pull up and stop before getting close to the flag.

This means that you have to create a picture of the ball's flight and roll in your mind's eye *before* you choose your club.

The chip-and-run grip
Holding the club correctly and aiming the club head towards the intermediate target are probably the least exciting parts of golf, but they are absolutely the most important. If you don't hold the club correctly, aim it correctly and stand correctly to the ball, your chances of a successful shot are very slight indeed.

We have shown already the standard golfing grip in detail (pp. 22 – 3) and this is the grip that is used for the chip-and-run shot, *except* that the hands are further down the shaft, giving you greater control.

The chip-and-run

1. The ball is lying well on top of the grass, 3 ft (1 m) from the edge of the green, and there is a further 33 ft (10 m) to the flag.

2. Choose your intermediate target and visualise the trajectory, the landing spot, the bounce and the roll of the ball towards the flag.

3. Hold the club further down the grip than normal. Open the stance slightly, with most of your weight on the left foot. Note the triangle formed by arms and shoulder line. (*Left*)

4. Take your practice swings to give you a feel for the amount of movement required to send the ball the correct distance. Visualise a successful result. (*Above*)

5. Address the ball and repeat your practice swing in 'reality', striking the ball with a crisp pendulum movement.

6. The follow through is the same length as, but slightly lower than, the backswing. The triangle remains the same throughout.

Stance

Place the club head on the ground, flat on its sole and with the club face aimed at the intermediate target. Be sure that the shaft is straight (your hands neither in front of nor behind the ball). Then take your stance in the following way.

1 With your feet the same distance apart as for the putt, keep your knees flexed, the toes of both feet swivelled very slightly to your left and your weight mainly on the left foot. Move your arms, hands and shaft so that they are in front of the ball and ensure that you have a straight line from your left shoulder through your left arm and shaft to the club head. Check to see that the club face still points towards the intermediate target.

2 Now open the stance a little by moving the left foot back 3 – 4 in (8 – 10 cm). This turns the lower part of your body slightly towards the target; this, together with the flexed knees and the weight on the left foot, helps to ensure a downward blow that strikes the ball first and then the grass, creating the desired trajectory.

Important!

When you open the stance, only the *lower* part of the body (feet, knees and hips) should be turned slightly towards the target, *absolutely not* your chest, shoulders and eyeline. These must remain parallel to the target line. Otherwise, you will not be aiming the shot correctly.

Posture

With knees flexed and pointing a little towards the target, weight on the left foot and with a shortened grip, the hands should be in front of the left thigh and just above the knee.

Those parts of the body nearest the target (left arm, hip and shoulder and the left side of the face) should be in front of the ball, which is centred between the feet.

The beginner will find this position tiring, so don't practise it for too long.

Every few minutes, stand up straight, stretch and rest a little.

When you have adopted the correct posture, the left arm and the club shaft will form one side of a triangle. The other side is formed by the right forearm, and the third by a line between the shoulders. This triangle should remain constant throughout the movement.

Movement

The movement is similar to that of putting, with the *arms only* creating the necessary amount of back-and-forward motion, and no wrist movement for the shorter chips. The distance the club head travels dictates the length the ball will fly and is the same on the backswing and on the follow through. This is sometimes difficult to see, as the club head on the follow through should finish closer to the ground than it was at the top of the backswing. This is due to the weight being mainly on the left foot.

Practise creating the pendulum movement with natural acceleration down to the ball, holding the finish position with the triangle intact and the club face pointing towards the target, ensuring that the weight is constant on the left foot and that the movement comes only from the arms.

With the experience gained from practising the chip-and-run, you will understand how the choice of club, the address position and backswing will affect the length and height of the shot, and the amount of roll after landing.

The chipping swing movement

1. The arms only create the swing, which is a pendulum movement. Shown here is the backswing. (*Above*)

2. On the follow through, the club head travels as much forwards as it did on the backswing – a true pendulum movement. (*Below*)

PRACTISING THE SHORT CHIP-AND-RUN SHOT

We show here an excellent way of practising your short chip-and-run shot, using tees to help you ensure that the ball is struck first (with a descending blow), thus creating the height necessary to land the ball just on the green and roll it up to the flag. Practising like this also helps you to understand the importance of keeping the triangle formed by the arms and shoulder line intact throughout the movement.

When you have practised in this way and you are satisfied with the success you have achieved, take a rest before changing the club and the target. Do not use any tees this time, but go through the illustrated routine once more, striking the ball first and the grass afterwards, keeping your triangle intact.

When you feel that you have mastered this, the next phase in your step-by-step approach to successful chipping is playing the same shot from the same position and to the same target but with different clubs, to gauge the difference in the results obtained and to gain experience of the trajectory and length of roll of each club. In other words, you must learn how far each club will fly the ball and how far the ball will roll after landing, given that you strike the ball with exactly the same movement.

Do not neglect practice from sloping positions too. A downhill lie requires a more lofted club, and vice versa. Side-slope shots should also be practised; you will find your practice swings immensely helpful in determining the point of contact between club and ground, and the direction the ball takes.

Practising the short chip and run _____

Drills for the short chip-and-run

3 x 3 balls
All balls to be the same distance from the edge of the green. First three from a good lie. Next three from a mediocre lie with a more lofted club. Last three from a bad lie and with an even more lofted club. Repeat the last three using the putter. Compare the results. Would it have been better to use the putter in this situation? (*See* page 36.)

You will see that the worse the lie, the more lofted the club should be.

3 x 3 balls Uphill lie
Use a club with *less* loft than you would choose if on an even lie.

3 x 3 balls Downhill lie
Use a club with *more* loft than you would choose if on an even lie.

3 x 3 balls
Play on to an upward-sloping green using a *less* lofted club.

3 x 3 balls
Play on to a downward-sloping green using a *more* lofted club.

3 x 3 balls Side-hill lies
Take extra care with your practice swings to determine where the club comes into contact with the ground. Note that if the ball is higher than your feet, it tends to go left of target, and vice versa.

1. Tee up about six balls and with a No. 8 iron play them at a specific target. Make sure that you strike the ball with a descending blow and that you make contact with the tee, knocking it over.

2. When you have been successful in striking both ball and tee every time, play them again, but this time with the tees lying on the ground about 2 in (5 cm) in front of the balls.

3. Striking the ball first and the tee afterwards is proof that you have struck the ball with a descending blow. Remember to think as well of the length of shot you want to play – all your successful shots should end up in the target area.

4. Only when you have gone through these steps successfully should you move on to practising the chip without a peg. Play the ball from the grass and remember to strike the ball first and then the grass. Never try to scoop the ball up in the air, just let the loft of the club do its work and the ball will lift correctly.

THE LONG CHIP-AND-RUN SHOT

When you are some 30 – 40 yds/m from the front edge of a long green with the flag well at the back, or if the green is double-tiered, your best bet could well be a long chip shot. The ball should fly fairly low, land well on the green and roll up to the flag. A high-trajectory ball flight is not only more difficult to judge when playing into a long green, but is more difficult to execute than the simple chip.

The choice of club

Even if the ball has a perfect lie, experience is the only thing that will help you here, as the distance to the green, compared to the distance to the flag, must be considered. A No. 8 or a No. 9 iron could be correct considering the distance the ball must travel in the air, compared to the distance it must cover on the ground.

Grip

Place your hands on the shaft as for the short chip-and-run shot, but higher up on the grip, because more movement is now needed to create the added distance required. About 1 1/2 in (4 cm) from the top is usually sufficient.

Stance

Take your stance only after you have visualised the shot and then seen a successful result with your practice swings. As always, the routine should be the same, the club placed behind the ball first, with the club face pointing directly at the intermediate target before you take your stance. As the distance you want the ball to travel increases, so does the distance between your feet. Keep your stance slightly open, with the weight favouring the left foot and more towards the balls of the feet. The ball should be back in the stance and the left arm and club shaft should be in a straight line.

Remember that it is only the lower part of the body that is open (turned to the left), not the shoulders or eyeline; otherwise the ball will very likely follow the shoulder line and finish considerably to the left of the target.

The long chip-and-run shot _____

1. The ball is lying well some 30 yds/m from the front edge of the green and the flag some 55 yds/m away.

2. Take a practice swing without the club, visualising the trajectory and length required for a successful shot. This helps you pick the right club for the shot, in this case a No. 9 iron.

3. Follow your normal pre-shot routine, feeling how the lengthened practice swing causes weight transference and a change of knee position.

4. Then play the ball in exactly the same way as your successful practice swings, which gave you the right feeling for the length of shot required.

5. When you have played your shot, hold the finish position and watch the result. This aids feedback, which increases your understanding that length of swing and choice of club affect both the length and trajectory of the shot.

Posture

The head should be over the ball and the hands well in front of it. Flex the knees because the increased movement on the backswing will cause a slight weight transference from left to right on the backswing and from right to left (but more so) on the downswing.

Movement

Although the swing is taken with the arms, the weight of the club head may cause the wrists to break slightly if the backswing is long enough. But the long chip is primarily an arm swing, distinct and robust, sending the ball fairly low before it lands on the putting surface, its trajectory and forward momentum sending it after two or three bounces rolling up to the flag. The amount of forward swing encourages the knees to follow, so that even more weight is on the left foot at the finish of the swing than at the address, and your right heel is slightly raised at the finish position.

PRACTISING THE LONG CHIP-AND-RUN SHOT

This type of shot is often called for during a round of golf, so your game will benefit if you practise it regularly. For some reason, many golfers consider this an easy shot, so their concentration is not always as sharp as it should be, resulting in poor visualisation and a lack of success. When they have a difficult chip to play, they concentrate more, and their improved visualisation as a rule leaves the ball only 2 or 3 yds/m from the flag. But the normal long chip-and-run shot, easy as it seems to execute, needs the same sharpness, otherwise you will find yourself too far from the flag to have a reasonable chance of finishing off with a single putt.

Therefore, always use your imagination before choosing the club and type of shot to be played. Use the same pre-shot routine as always; seeing a successful result with your practice swing is a must.

Vary the lie of the ball, not forgetting uphill and downhill shots. Compete with yourself and see how many times out of ten the ball lands in the chosen area and how many times it rolls the correct distance. Vary your choice of club and swing length in order to create feedback. Remember this is the golf swing in miniature. The correct execution of this shot will enhance your chances of swinging the club correctly when you come to use the half, three-quarter and full swing movements.

Practising the two-levered chip

Taking about ten balls on to the practice ground, pick a suitable target area where you want the ball to land if you play it with your No. 9 iron. In this example, the area is about 25 yds (23 m) away.

1. Take your practice swings to gauge the length of swing required to play the ball 25 yds (23 m).

2. The address position with the No. 9 iron: ball in the centre of the stance, weight favouring the left side, and hands just in front of the ball. Light grip pressure.

3. On the backswing, the wrists cock slightly due to the light grip and the length of the swing.

4. The ball is struck and on its way. Note how the triangle formed by the arms and shoulder line is maintained all the way.

5. Hold the follow-through position to get feedback concerning the length of swing you used to achieve this shot length. Note how this photo is a perfect copy of the practice swing in photo 1, opposite, except that the ball is well on its way to the target area.

won't hinge your wrists too much on the backswing), thus preventing the ball from flying too high.

Stance

Because you are using a longer club, the swing will be shorter, so the feet do not need to be so far apart as they would be for the full swing movement. Keep your weight more on the left foot than on the right. The ball is just right of centre and your hands should be in front of it.

Posture

Your posture depends very much on the distance you want to hit the ball, on pre-vailing wind conditions, and on your choice of club. The shorter grip causes you to stand nearer the ball with just a little knee flex. Keep your weight forwards on the balls of the feet (but more on the left foot than on the right) and the hips pointed slightly left of target (which tends to keep the movement firm and prevents the backswing being too long).

Movement

Swing the club low and wide on the backswing. The firmness of the grip will ensure that the wrists bend less than usual. The half backswing will take the arms to the nine o'clock position, while the three-quarter swing will take them to the ten o'clock position. On the downswing the club is returned to the ball with the left arm pulling close to the body in order to keep the club head on an inside path and behind the hands. The swing is very controlled and the finish position on the follow through (three o'clock or two o'clock) is a copy of the backswing.

The half and three-quarter swings are identical, apart from the length of the backswing and the follow through. You must decide yourself which of these partial shots to play, as the amount of movement required is dictated by how hard and from what direction the wind is blowing, by the distance you want the ball to fly, and by your choice of club.

3. Just after impact, the arms are swinging towards the target and the ball is on its way. The upper body is relatively still, while the club moves back to the inside of the target line.

4. A controlled finish, with the weight on the left foot and the right heel leaving the ground late in the follow through and the arms ending in the two o'clock position.

The three-quarter swing from a good lie

1. The ball has a good lie, some 90 yds (80 m) from the green and 30 yds (27 m) more to the flag, which is at the back of a long, upward-sloping green. A No. 6 or No. 7 iron is the right club for this particular shot.

2. Following the usual pre-swing routine, pick out the intermediate target and take your established number of practice swings to get the proper feel for the shot. (Compare this with photo 6 on the opposite page: the actual swing is an exact copy of the practice swing.)

3. Having completed your pre-swing routine, address the ball. Then using mainly your arms, take a wide three-quarter backswing, with the left heel on the ground and with your hands firm on the shaft to prevent too much wrist movement.

4. With left arm and side very much in control, swing the club back to the ball, arms leading and with the left arm close to the body to ensure a swing from the inside. *(Above)*

5. Arms flowing wide out to the target before moving inside and up to the three-quarter position. The finger pressure reduces wrist movement and keeps the ball low. *(Above right)*

6. When you have completed the follow through, your arms, hands and club should have the same position as they had on the backswing. Body weight well on the left foot and right knee turned inwards towards the target, causing your right heel to leave the ground. *(Right)*

A PARTIAL SWING FROM A DIVOT MARK

This shot is also known as the 'punch' shot.

If the ball is lying badly on the fairway (for instance, in a divot mark), you can play a punch shot to ensure that you strike the ball well. The punch shot is the same as the half or three-quarter swing just described, except that you stop the club early on in the follow through.

Be sure that your hands are in front of the ball at impact and that the arms, not the wrists, are used. The club should stop pointing at the target, with the toe of the club head pointing at the sky. Using the wrists in this shot, together with the early stop on the follow through, would result in the ball curving to the left in the air.

The punch shot, although not the easiest of shots to play, should be a part of your golfing arsenal. It can be used when playing from under trees, from bad lies and when playing from an elevated tee into a strong headwind. The correct choice of club, together with a strong but unhurried arm swing, will send the ball low and with plenty of roll.

It is vital that you use the arms only so as to prevent the club face closing before the ball is struck. As in all strong shots, if the club is stopped soon after impact, the ball may turn left in the air; so, be sure to practise the shot on the practice ground before playing it on the course.

Partial shots are not only the absolutely correct shot to play on certain occasions, but they also teach us that out on the golf course it is not always necessary to play a shot that makes you feel that you must exert yourself unduly.

Many weekend players would benefit if they played more three-quarter controlled shots instead of playing an exaggerated full swing movement at top speed.

Playing from a divot mark

1. The ball is lying in a divot mark on the fairway, making clean contact difficult. It is 120 yds (110 m) from the flag, which is again at the far end of a long green. A headwind causes further difficulty.

2. Choose your No. 6 iron. This will become a No. 5 iron when you have your hands in front of the ball and the ball is back in the stance. Take your practice swings as usual.

3. A half to three-quarter backswing with reduced wrist movement will allow you to get at the ball better when it is lying this badly.

4. A solid and unhurried movement through the ball, with the arms leading all the way, will send the ball low towards the target, bouncing before reaching the green and rolling up to the flag.

5. The right arm has added the necessary thrust and the hands are passive all the way. The arms are stretched and the shaft points towards the target, with the toe of the club pointing towards the sky and the left hip turned well out of the way.

CHAPTER SEVEN
THE FULL SWING

The full swing movement, properly carried out, will achieve optimum distance and direction with every club. It does not mean hitting the ball with full power. The swing movement is basically the same no matter which club you use, the only difference being that the swing plane is most upright for the No. 9 iron and least upright for the driver. The reasons are the length of shaft, the lie of the club, and the position of the ball in the stance. With the longer clubs, these factors will automatically cause you to stand further away from the ball, more upright, and with more upper body behind the ball. The further you stand from the ball, the flatter the swing will be, thus creating a shallower arc through the hitting area and sending the ball further.

Every club in your bag will give you a certain distance when the ball is struck correctly at a controlled speed with the same swing movement. Remember it is the target area that is important: a well played shot with a longer club will always give a better result than if you take a shorter club and force the swing in the vain hope of creating added length. Each change of club to a lower number will send the ball between 10 and 15 yds/m further, so try to swing every club at the same speed: avoid the trap of trying to hit the longer clubs harder.

For most people, 75% power with a complete swing movement will always give the best results. You never really need full power.

The full golf swing is the movement made when the club choice alone decides the height and length of the shot played. In other words, each individual golfer should have only one full swing movement; the different heights and lengths that he or she can achieve with this movement are dictated by the club used.

The important thing to remember about the full swing is that it is a fluid movement, not the moving of your club through a number of different positions. One thousand different positions will not create a successful golf swing, but the golf swing moves smoothly through a thousand positions!

Your pre-swing routine for all full swing shots is also the same, but your stance, posture and ball position will differ slightly, being dictated by your build, your personal swing and the length of club you have chosen for the shot.

Two very important factors should dominate the average golfer's use of the full swing: the first is that you must have a good mental picture of the shot to be played; the second is that you should always make a conservative choice of club. As you cannot expect to hit every shot 100%, you ought to choose a club that will reach the target when you swing comfortably within your capacity.

PRE-SWING ROUTINE

Do not take practice swings when you play the full swing movement. There are three reasons for this.

1 The full swing movement is too tiring.

2 After every full swing it takes time for the muscles to return to normal. It would delay the game unnecessarily and destroy your rhythm if you had to wait the required time after each practice swing.

3 The full swing movement is the same length every time, so there is little need to gauge the length of the backswing.

However, this does not mean that you must omit your pre-shot routine. It must be followed, with the following change.

After deciding that you need to play a full swing, pick out the intermediate target. Then make two or three 'mini-swings' (not more than one-quarter swings) at a slow pace, seeing all the while in your mind's eye the perfect flight, bounce and roll of the ball.

Now, before taking your stance, place the club head correctly behind the ball.

The full swing routine

1. First choose the target area. Which line will it take and how far can it be expected to fly? Once the line is picked out, the intermediate target is chosen.

A couple of preliminary waggles help you to sharpen up, then a forward press leads you smoothly into the backswing, in which the left hand and arm move the club head back and up. With the shorter irons, it is not necessary to have the shaft pointing straight at the target (parallel to the target line) at the top of the backswing, provided that the shoulders are free from tension. With the longer clubs, this tends to happen automatically.

2. Place the club carefully behind the ball, which is teed so that half of it is above the top of the club head, which in turn must be aligned directly with the intermediate target.

3. The stance is now taken and the feet and body are adjusted to the club and the ball.

4. The waggle brings the club head back along the swing path at the pace at which you are going to make the backswing. Remember, always make the same number of waggles.

5. The club is returned to the ball and the forward press is made, the right knee moving slightly in towards the left knee and the hands moving just past the ball.

6. The arms swing the club back from the ball in a low, wide arc at the same pace as the waggle.

7. A full, free swing with the arms causes the shoulders to turn and the weight to shift to the inside of the right foot. The left knee is pulled to the right, causing the left heel to lift.

8. As the left arm swings the club down on the inside, the weight shifts naturally back to the left foot.

9. Just after impact, the arms swing out after the ball, the left hip moving out of the way and the head slightly further back and lower than it was at address, due to the movement of the lower body.

10. The right side and shoulder are coming through and under, while the head has not yet moved.

11. The correct finish position: well balanced, the right foot perpendicular and the belt buckle pointing at the target.

Change of swing plane

In a correctly executed golf swing, there is a noticeable change of swing plane between the backswing and the downswing. (Swing plane, as we have said, is the angle of the swing arc to the ground.) The club is swung back from the ball and then inside the target line and up. However, it does not return to the ball on the same plane, but rather on a flatter plane, caused by the leg and hip movement to the left at the same time as the arms pull the club down on the inside.

1. The backswing position with a middle iron. The weight is on the right foot, the shaft is parallel with the target line and in the correct plane. The club face is correctly positioned.

2. The downswing is under way, with the weight moving on to the left foot and the lower body turning as the club is pulled down on the inside of the target line, creating a flatter plane.

3. After the strike, the weight is on the left foot, the hips have moved through the shot, the right knee into the left, and the arms swing inside and across the chest, while the upper body is still well back.

4. The follow through is completed. The arms are well round to the inside, pulling the body into a position where the weight is on the left heel, with the right foot perpendicular and the shoulders fully square to the target.

Swing plane

Illustrated here are the address positions and the consequent backswings for four different clubs. You can see from these photos that the nearer you stand to the ball, the more you bend forwards and the more upright is the backswing. Furthermore, the shorter irons cause a more downward blow, while the longer clubs (which have the ball forwards in the stance) have a shallower downward angle and a more forward movement into the hitting area.

1. Address position with the No. 9 iron: close to the ball.

2. Backswing with the No. 9 iron. The swing is quite upright.

3. Address position with the No. 6 iron: less close to the ball.

4. Backswing with the No. 6 iron. The swing is less upright.

5. Address position with the No. 4 iron: further from the ball.

6. Backswing with the No. 4 iron. Swing is flatter.

7. Address position with the No. 3 wood: furthest from the ball.

8. Backswing with the No. 3 wood. Swing is flattest.

THE FULL SWING WITH THE SHORT IRONS

The short irons (the Nos 7, 8 and 9 irons) are used when accuracy is at a premium. The ball should be struck just before the bottom of the swing arc, with a steeply descending club head. The line that the club head follows in the forward swing is down from the inside to along (where contact takes place) to inside, and up at the finish.

Due to the fact that the short irons are shorter-shafted and more lofted, play them with a different stance and posture than you adopt when playing the longer clubs. Standing nearer the ball creates a more upright plane, with less body movement and with the feeling that it is mostly the arms and hands that are employed during the swing. This type of swing produces an air of great authority and crispness. The ball is struck first, and then the ground, taking turf.

The full swing movement with the short irons is still primarily a precision shot because the amount of back-spin helps to keep the ball on line. The pitching wedge should never be used for a full swing (greater accuracy can be achieved more easily with the No. 9 iron and a three-quarter swing). The short irons are fairly easy to use and are therefore popular with all golfers.

Grip

The grip used for the full swing with the short irons is the normal one, but the club is never held at the extreme end of the shaft. Depending on the lie and the height required, the clubs are held lower down on the shaft.

Stance

Since the arm movement is now a full swing, which turns the shoulders, bringing your weight more on to the inside edge of the right foot during the backswing, the feet must be far enough apart and slightly open to allow for all this extra movement

The full swing with the short irons

When playing the short irons, it is not enough just to aim at the green: here you are going for the flag. Precision is the key word.

1. The stance is marginally open and rather narrow, with just a fraction more weight on the right foot. Because you are standing near the ball, the swing will be upright.

2. The backswing is very controlled – primarily an arm and hand movement – but wide and long enough to bring the weight on to the inside of the right foot.

4. With the stance taken, check that the club is still in the correct position and that your eyeline, shoulders, hips, knees and feet are parallel to the target line.

5. Preparatory to starting the backswing, make your usual number of waggles, at the speed at which you intend to start the backswing.

6. The ball is struck and on its way. Hips have moved out of the way to the left to allow the arms to continue from the target line to the inside before moving up.

7. The swing is completed by a well balanced and fully relaxed follow through.

CHAPTER EIGHT
THE SAND GAME

The sand shot is often considered the toughest of them all. No matter how well you play golf, you cannot avoid getting into sand now and then. It may be due to an unlucky bounce or you may simply have played a bad shot – it makes no difference, you still have to play the ball out of that bunker!

The object of shots from the sand is always the same: to see to it that the next shot is as simple as possible and to try to avoid losing a stroke.

It is essential that you practise sand shots as often as you can. Practice will give you experience; from experience you will gain knowledge. To play sand shots successfully, you must know how the club functions as it works its way through the sand and how the ball will fly when you 'splash' both sand and ball into the air. This knowledge will help you to approach any normal bunker shot with confidence.

The sand iron is different from the other irons. If you use an ordinary iron to play a shot from soft sand, it will dig in and stop abruptly, leaving the ball in the sand. The sand iron is built to bounce through the sand, displacing and compressing it behind the ball so that the sand and ball are 'splashed' into the air. Don't hit the ball, hit the sand. Furthermore, the sand cushions the power of the swing, so that the ball comes out softly.

When the shaft is upright, the trailing edge (also known as the 'flange' or 'bounce') of the sole is lower than the leading edge, enabling the club to bounce through the sand. This distinguishes the sand iron from all the other clubs. With its average loft of 56°, it is the most lofted of all clubs, enabling you to play quickly-rising, high shots.

The sand iron

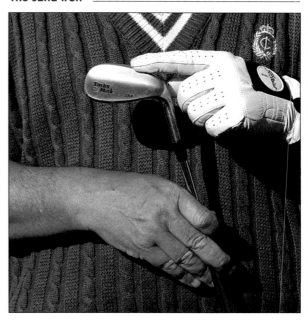

1. The sole of the sand iron is much wider than that of the other clubs and is noticeably convex. (Remember that the sand iron can be used to advantage in other situations too, e.g. in the rough.)

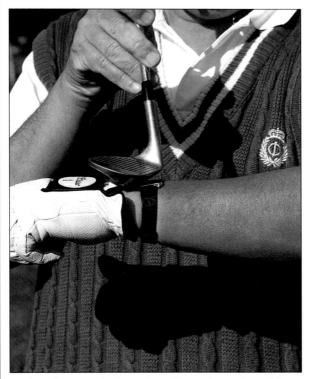

2. This photograph shows how the trailing edge of the sole is closer to the ground than is the leading edge. The more the club is opened, the lower the trailing edge will be and the easier it will bounce through the sand.

3. When the club is open the shaft is nearer the ball and there is a danger of hitting it with the hosel. To avoid this, address the ball off the toe of the club, as shown.

A GOOD LIE IN A GREENSIDE BUNKER WITH NORMAL SAND

Learn how to play this shot so that the ball finishes close to the flag and you will save many strokes.

Grip

Except for one very important difference, hold the club with the normal grip about 2 – 3 in (50 – 75 mm) down the shaft. The essential difference is that the club face is not square to the target, but open (i.e., turned to the right), and this is done before you place the hands on the club. Do this before you get into the sand bunker because you need to ground the club in the open position before you can place the hands on the shaft properly.

Opening the club face lowers the trailing edge even more, causing the club to bounce through the sand instead of digging in. The ball will be propelled then by the displacement of the sand behind it, softly, slowly, and with a considerable amount of height, ensuring that the ball stops shortly after landing.

Stance

Plant the feet securely in the sand with your whole body aligned to the left of the target – that is, with an open stance. This stance, when combined with the open club face, will create the height that the ball flies. The more the feet are aligned to the

From a good lie in a greenside bunker with normal sand

1. When you open the blade to create more bounce and height, you must do it outside the bunker and before you actually grip the shaft. Otherwise, there is a danger that the blade will return to square before impact.

2. Take your practice swings outside the bunker too, because you may not ground the club in the sand (two-stroke penalty!). The practice swings give you the right feel for the swing and allow you to visualise the successful result.

left and the more the club face is open (aligned to the right), the higher and shorter the ball will travel.

When you have learned to face your whole body the same angle to the left as the club face is pointing to the right, control of distance becomes easier.

Keep your weight centred, with the ball in line with the left heel and addressed towards the toe of the sand iron. When playing, do not ground the club in the bunker. When first practising this shot, lay your club head softly on the sand, as this will increase your confidence. (If you hold the club in the air from the beginning, it is difficult to know where to strike the sand.)

Posture

Keep the knees flexed and the body relaxed. The hands should be hanging freely from the shoulders, very slightly in front of the ball, and the club should not, of course, touch the sand.

Swing movement

The grip, stance and posture promote a swing that will take a long, shallow 'divot' of sand and compress it behind the ball, propelling it out of the bunker. The swing itself is very upright, rather long, and very much slower than you would expect necessary. Watch professionals playing this shot and you will think that they are trying to

From a good lie in a greenside bunker with normal sand, cont.

3. Ball in line with the left instep; feet, hips and shoulders point to left of target as much as club is open to right; weight centred. The ball is towards the toe of the club.

4. With a light grip and an early wrist break, take a full, free backswing. The tempo should be easy throughout. Leg action on the backswing is minimal. Left arm/hand dominates as usual.

play in slow motion. The line of the swing follows the stance – that is, to the left of the target. The arms lead the downswing all the way. The ball will come out of the bunker about halfway between where you have swung the club and where the blade was pointing when the club hit the sand.

Until you are proficient at this, it is a good idea to follow through to a high finish by concentrating on continuing the movement of the left side, with a distinct feeling of pulling the left arm to the left. This will stop the right hand from taking over and closing the club face, which should be pointing to the sky until near the end of the swing.

Even when playing very short shots, with the flag close to the edge of the bunker, it is better in the beginning to play the high follow through with a slower swing to be certain of getting out of the bunker and on to the green. Eventually, when you have gained enough confidence, you can stop the club earlier and lower to the ground, reducing the distance the ball travels.

5. Just after impact. The compressed sand is 'splashed' out of the bunker, lifting the ball high and softly over the front lip of the bunker.

6. The full follow through should leave you in a well balanced position. Swing exactly as if it were a normal golf shot. The result: perfect! All that is left is a simple putt.

FROM HARD SAND IN A GREENSIDE BUNKER

This type of sand shot differs from the others insofar as you should hit the ball first and not the sand.

If rain has packed the sand in a bunker, the sand iron will bounce on the surface rather than go into the sand. This means that the ball will be struck halfway up, making it hit the wall of the bunker or fly low and hard over the green. The trailing edge will not move any sand at all if the sand is hard, so you must avoid striking the sand before making contact with the ball. Therefore, don't choose a sand iron but take the pitching wedge instead and use a similar shot to the short pitch over a bunker. (Go back to Chapter Five and compare – there are many similarities.) The idea is the same, too – to 'pinch' the ball at the very bottom of the swing.

Grip
Hold the pitching wedge 2 in (5 cm) down on the shaft, with firm pressure from both hands but slightly more coming from the left fingers. Check that the blade is square with the intermediate target and close to the base of the ball (but not touching it or the sand).

Stance
Stand with about 8 – 10 in (20 – 25 cm) between the feet so that the ball is centred in the stance. The feet should be slightly open (pointing a little towards the intermediate target).

Posture
Flex the knees very slightly and hold the club with the hands directly over the ball.

Swing movement
Take a short backswing, about chest high, with very early wrist break to create a steep and high backswing arc. The downswing is initiated by pulling the club down with the left arm, the right arm passing in a flipping action directly under the stretched left arm shortly after impact. Allow the right knee to follow the swing to ensure that there will be increased weight on the left foot. Because the body is virtually still and the follow through is curtailed, the ball is pinched, giving it plenty of back-spin to stop it quickly after landing.

This shot, although appearing to be slow and lazy, creates a great deal of its effect by the fact that the ball is struck by the club and not by the sand. The hit-and-stop action, with the right hand flipping under the stretched left arm, imparts back-spin, so even if the ball comes out strongly, it will stop very soon after landing.

Short pitch from packed sand

Make practice swings outside the bunker, as you are not allowed to touch the ground in a bunker.

1. Hold the pitching wedge firmly, with a shortened grip. The club blade is near the base of the ball. Your weight is centred, stance slightly open and hands directly above the ball.

2. Break the wrists early to make a short, steep backswing. Your weight is still centred and your foot and knee positions are unaltered.

3. Pull the club down with the left arm, and at contact the ball is pinched due to the right hand passing under the stretched left arm.

4. The right knee is allowed to follow forwards, even though the club is stopped shortly after impact. This produces maximum spin.

PLAYING FROM A HALF-BURIED LIE IN A GREENSIDE BUNKER

Should the ball be half-buried in the sand, you may very easily get too much sand between the club head and the ball, or your club head may bounce and strike the top of the ball. Both these shots would leave the ball in the sand. To avoid this, you need to make some adjustments.

When the ball is lying half-buried, two things are necessary. At impact, there must be less sand than usual between the club face and the ball, and the club head must penetrate deeper into the sand. In other words, the club should not bounce through the sand but should dig into it.

Grip

Although you use the normal grip, you now want the club face to be square or closed (depending on the texture of the sand and how deep the ball is in it). Hold the club more firmly than usual about 2 in (5 cm) down the shaft.

Stance

The stance is square, with the feet firmly anchored in the sand to prevent slipping. With the blade square and the ball well inside the left heel, keep your weight predominantly on the left foot.

Posture

The shot is much more aggressive than the normal sand shot; therefore the knees and arms are less relaxed (don't allow any slackness to creep in). The hands and upper body are well in front of the ball, which results in a very steep entry into the sand.

Swing movement

Swing the club back from the ball steeply by cocking the wrists as early as possible on the backswing. On the downswing, swing the club with the hands and wrists so that the club enters the sand just behind the ball, popping it out.

This swing is short, sharp and direct, with body weight on the left foot throughout the whole movement. The deep penetration of the sand curtails the

The half-buried lie

1. After practice swings outside the bunker (with square blade), address the half-buried ball with it well inside your left heel, and your club face and feet square to the intermediate target. Your weight favours the left foot. Hands are in front of the ball.

follow through and the club often stops in the sand.

A lie such as this can be frightening for the faint-hearted, but don't let it put you off – simply remember the following. The downswing is very steep so there won't be much sand between club head and ball to soften the effect. This means that the ball will come out lower and faster than for a good lie (*see* above). Therefore, when you strike the sand near the ball don't apply so much force, otherwise it will come out too far and will roll a considerable distance as well.

2. An earlier wrist break and a firmer grip than for the good-lie shot. Use plenty of wrist when swinging the club head steeply down into the sand just behind the ball.

3. At impact, the sand propels the ball softly over the intermediate target and on to the green, where it rolls towards the flag. The square blade and firmer grip have 'splashed' the sand and ball up into the air.

Remember that this shot produces more roll because of the increased amount of sand between club face and ball.

THE BURIED LIE

Should the ball be almost completely buried, as it can easily be if the sand is soft and the ball comes in from a high trajectory, make a few slight adjustments to the way you handled the half-buried lie.

Grip

First, close the club before taking your grip, with the toe of the club nearly pointing at the ball and with the hands directly over it. Hold the club quite firmly and a good 3 in (75 mm) down the shaft.

Stance

The ball should be back of centre in the stance, which should be closed – that is, the right foot is drawn back about 8 – 10 in (20 – 25 cm). Your weight should be well on the left foot.

Posture

Keep the knees and arms less relaxed than normal, with the upper body and hands well in front of the ball.

Swing movement

Start the swing by cocking the wrists immediately at the beginning of a short, abrupt backswing. Hit down into the sand at the very back of the ball. The club will have displaced sufficient sand to send the ball out of the bunker, often leaving the club head still in the sand.

Once again, the ball will come out low and without back-spin, so if there is a high bank in front of the buried ball, play out of the bunker where the lip is low enough to ensure that the ball does not remain in the bunker.

The buried lie in a greenside bunker

1. The ball has landed in the bunker from a high trajectory and is plugged in soft sand.

2. Take the stance outside the bunker with the club face closed. Then place your hands about 3 in (75 mm) down the club shaft. Your toe line should point as much to the right as the club face is pointing to the left. Make practice swings as usual.

3. Now, retaining this grip, go into the bunker and adopt the same stance. Work the feet deep into the sand to give balance. The soles of the shoes should be below the level of the ball. (*Above*)

4. A short and very upright backswing with lots of wrist cock and a stable foot position starts off the swing movement. (*Above right*)

5. Swing the closed club head on a steep path into the sand just behind the ball. Hit down and let the wrists and club do the work. Be prepared for considerable roll, as the ball will have very little back-spin.

PUTTING FROM THE SAND

If the ball is lying on packed sand and there is no lip to the bunker, you may be able to putt the ball out with considerable accuracy. Everything is exactly the same as when you putt from off the green (Chapter Two), with sufficient movement to be sure to come out of the bunker. Don't try to hit the ball harder; if you do, you will end up striking it badly. Remember, it is the length of the backswing that should dictate the length the ball will travel.

Putting from the sand is not difficult if you remember the following. Take your practice swings outside the bunker in order to judge the length of swing required to ensure that the ball rolls out of the bunker.

Use the normal putting grip. Keep the hands and weight well forwards to the left, with the body absolutely still. The practice swings will have told you how long a backswing you need.

Follow your usual putting routine, but don't ground the club, and be sure to make the swing with your body still and your eye on the back of the ball.

Putting from the sand

1. Take your practice swings outside the bunker, gauging the length of backswing needed. It will be rather longer than you imagined – you do not want to increase the speed of the swing or move on the forward swing. (*Below left*)

2. Take up your stance with the weight mainly on the left foot and the hands in front of the ball. Address the ball one-third of the way up to avoid touching the sand. (*Below right*)

3. Be sure to repeat the long backswing of your practice swing. Do not hurry the downswing but maintain a smooth rhythm, keeping the body still and the eyes on the back of the ball.

4. Strike the ball with a smooth forward movement, keeping the head still and the eyes on where the ball was until well after the strike.

5. The ball has rolled up the bank of hard sand and continued to finish near the flag. A wise decision has saved you a stroke.

SHOTS FROM FAIRWAY BUNKERS

As your golf improves and you start sending the ball further from the tee, you might find yourself in a fairway bunker, still some considerable distance from the green. Should the lip of the bunker be fairly low (they usually are on fairway bunkers), your choice of club will depend on the lie of the ball and the distance required.

But a word of warning. No matter what club you use, it must have sufficient loft (even when you de-loft it by having your hands in front of the ball) to clear the front lip of the bunker. If the ball is still in the bunker after the shot, nine times out of ten it is because you have chosen a club that was not lofted enough. So choose your club with care. It is better to take a No. 7 iron and be 20 yds/m short of the green than to take a No. 5 iron and not get out of the bunker at all!

PLAYING AN IRON FROM A FAIRWAY BUNKER

If you have a bad lie in a fairway bunker, it is better to take the sand iron and 'splash' the ball safely back on to the fairway, rather than to take one of the other irons and go for length. However, if you have a decent lie choose a safe, lofted iron, say the No. 7.

Grip
Hold the club with the normal grip $1/2$ in (12 mm) from the top. Take your practice swings outside the bunker to create feel for the precision in strike necessary to hit the ball cleanly.

Iron shots from a fairway bunker

1. A No. 7 iron is a good choice for this kind of shot. Take the stance with hands in front of the ball, which is well back in the stance. The club face should be slightly open. The right foot is angled into the sand and the right knee is flexed inwards to assist stability.

2. The backswing is completed. The arms swing freely, while the weight is centred and the right knee position constant.

Stance

Take your stance as for a normal shot with a middle iron, with both feet planted securely in the sand, but with the right angled markedly inwards, so as to provide a solid base for the backswing. This is to stop you moving during the backswing.

Hold the club in the air, just behind the ball, with the aim slightly to the left because the weight on the left foot will cause the ball to turn right in the air. The ball is just back of centre to facilitate striking the ball without contacting the sand.

Posture

Keep the hands and arms in front of the ball and place your weight primarily on the left foot. Maintain the knees very slightly flexed, giving you the feeling that you are standing high.

Swing movement

The normal backswing will tend to be more upright than usual, because the hands are in front of the ball and your weight is more on the left foot. Therefore, the club head will not touch the sand as you bring it back from the address position.

The reduced knee flex and angled right foot position will assist you to stand stably during the backswing. The downswing should be unhurried, concentrating on striking the ball and taking as little sand as possible before continuing to a full, controlled and well-balanced follow through.

3. The ball is struck first and very little sand is taken, so that the arms continue up and to the inside, with the upper body still behind where the ball was positioned.

4. The follow through is completed. The weight is now on the left foot, the hips are turned to the target and balance and poise have been maintained through good rhythm.

WOOD SHOT FROM A FAIRWAY BUNKER

Should the ball be sitting very well and the sand be not too soft, it may be possible to use a lofted wooden club (the 4, 5 or 7 wood) from the bunker.

Grip
Make sure that the club head is open before taking your grip. Remember to take your practice swings outside the bunker to create feel for the shot you are about to play.

Stance
Plant the feet firmly in the sand, with the right foot angled inwards to assist stability. The ball is played slightly less forwards than usual, as the back edge of the club sole bounces on the sand at contact.

Posture
Stand high, with the knees only very slightly flexed and with your weight centred. Keep the hands in line with the ball, with the club open and, of course, not in contact with the sand.

Aim slightly to the left, as the open club face will cause the ball to curve to the right in the air.

Movement
Make a smooth and controlled backswing followed by an unhurried downswing that allows the club to bounce at impact on the back edge of its sole, as you continue to a full and well-balanced finish.

PLAYING WINNING SHOTS FROM THE SAND

As we said at the beginning of this chapter, courage and confidence are necessary with sand shots, and these will only increase if you practise regularly. You must be able to play bunker shots well enough to avoid losing a stroke, so be sure to spend at least some time every week in the practice bunker.

Wood shots from a fairway bunker

If the ball is lying well in a fairway bunker, the sand is not too soft and there is a low lip between the ball and the target, you may consider using a lofted wood.

1. With the ball in the centre of the stance, hold the club so that the face is open and not in contact with the sand. The right foot is angled strongly so that the inside presses into the sand.

The table opposite sums up the most important points in this chapter. It is a handy guide for quick reference when the ball has landed in normal sand in a greenside bunker and you are considering what to do. The table indicates what swing movement is required when playing from good, half-buried and buried lies.

Remember that you cannot ground your club in a sand bunker without being penalised, and the only way you can feel the texture of the sand is when you walk into the bunker and take your stance.

2. The backswing is slightly shorter and steeper than for a fairway wood shot due to the lack of leg movement (caused by the right ankle position).

3. The arms continue freely into the follow through, the weight being pulled over on to the left leg and the lower body turning towards the target.

Ready-reckoner for bunker play

LIE	STANCE	SWING
Good	Ball in line with left instep, club open, feet, hips and shoulder point to left as much as the club is open to the right. Weight centred.	Free, easy swing with plenty of wrist break. Full follow through. Light grip. 'Slow motion' swing.
Half-buried	Ball well inside the left heel, club and feet square to target. Weight favours left foot.	Free swing with wrists broken earlier than before. Firmer grip.
Buried	Ball back in the stance, club closed, feet, hips and shoulders point to right as much as club is closed to the left.	Firm, resolute grip, wrists break immediately, sharp downswing with right hand pushing into sand. The swing is a strong movement.